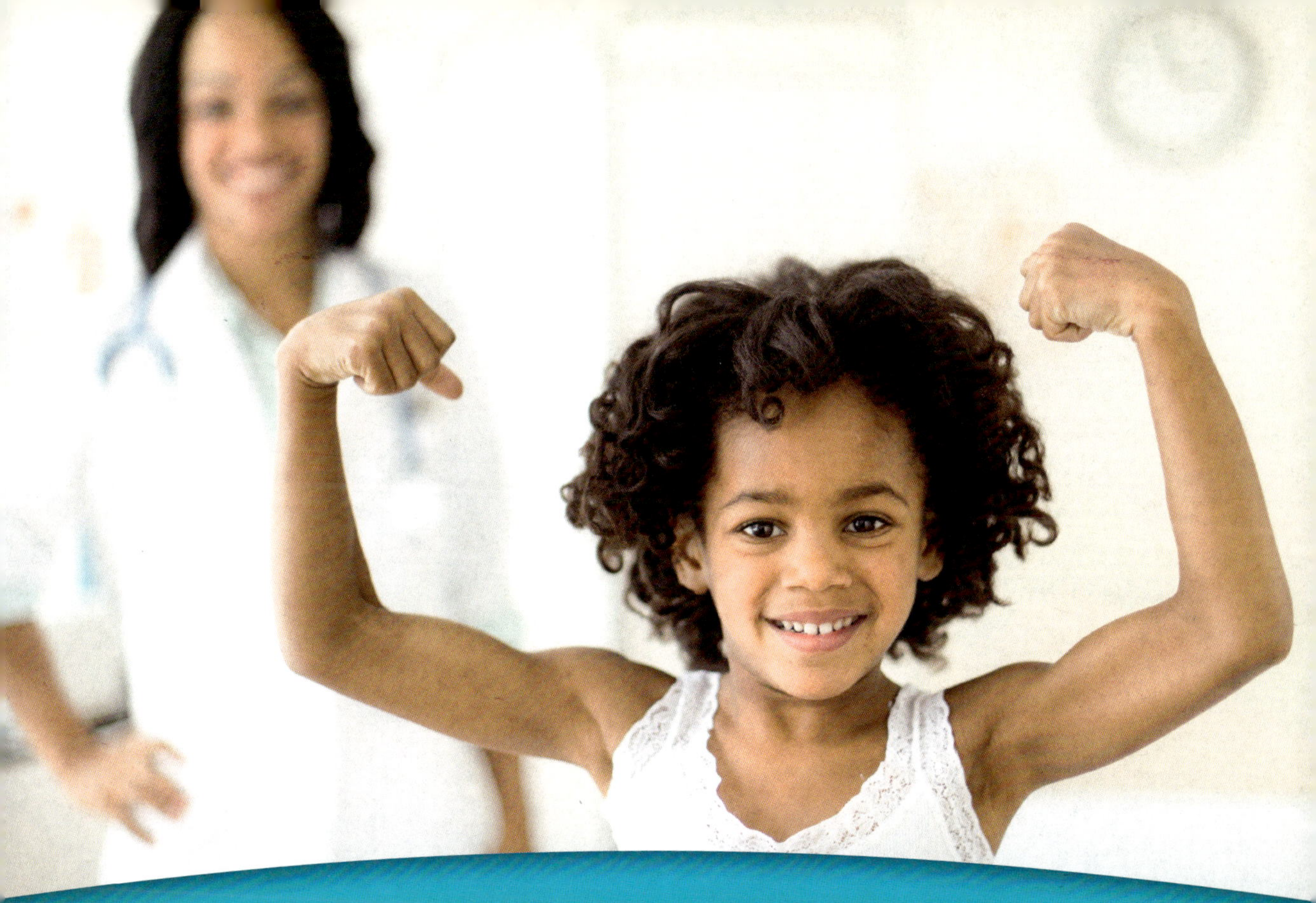

All About Your
MUSCLES

Jane P. Gardner and Maria Koran

www.av2books.com

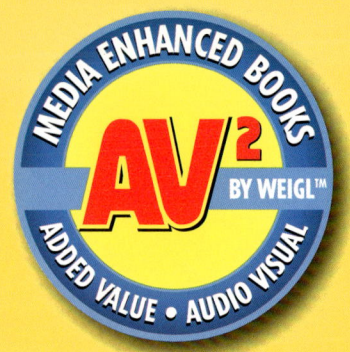

AV² provides enriched content that supplements and complements this book. Weigl's AV² books strive to create inspired learning and engage young minds in a total learning experience.

Your AV² Media Enhanced books come alive with...

 **Audio** Listen to sections of the book read aloud.

 **Key Words** Study vocabulary, and complete a matching word activity.

Go to www.av2books.com, and enter this book's unique code.

 **Video** Watch informative video clips.

 **Quizzes** Test your knowledge.

BOOK CODE

R523873

 **Embedded Weblinks** Gain additional information for research.

 **Slide Show** View images and captions, and prepare a presentation.

AV² by Weigl brings you media enhanced books that support active learning.

 **Try This!** Complete activities and hands-on experiments.

... and much, much more!

Published by AV² by Weigl
350 5th Avenue, 59th Floor
New York, NY 10118
Website: www.av2books.com

Copyright © 2017 AV² by Weigl
All rights reserved. No part of this publication may be reproduced, stored in a retrieval system, or transmitted in any form or by any means, electronic, mechanical, photocopying, recording, or otherwise, without the prior written permission of the publisher.

Library of Congress Cataloging-in-Publication Data

Names: Gardner, Jane P., author. | Koran, Maria, author.
Title: Muscles / Jane P. Gardner and Maria Koran.
Description: New York, NY : AV2 by Weigl, [2017] | Series: All about your... | Includes bibliographical references and index.
Identifiers: LCCN 2016034647 (print) | LCCN 2016035357 (ebook) | ISBN 9781489651464 (hard cover : alk. paper) | ISBN 9781489651471 (soft cover : alk. paper) | ISBN 9781489651488 (Multi-user ebk.)
Subjects: LCSH: Muscles--Juvenile literature.
Classification: LCC QP321 .G357 2017 (print) | LCC QP321 (ebook) | DDC 612.7/4--dc23
LC record available at https://lccn.loc.gov/2016034647

Printed in the United States of America in Brainerd, Minnesota
1 2 3 4 5 6 7 8 9 0 20 19 18 17 16

082016
210716

Project Coordinator: Piper Whelan   Art Director: Terry Paulhus

Every reasonable effort has been made to trace ownership and to obtain permission to reprint copyright material. The publishers would be pleased to have any errors or omissions brought to their attention so that they may be corrected in subsequent printings.

Weigl acknowledges Getty Images and Alamy as its primary image suppliers for this title.

Contents

AV² Book Code 2
Chapter 1 What Are Muscles? 4
Chapter 2 Muscle Types 8
Chapter 3 Problems with Muscles 12
Chapter 4 Keeping Your Muscles Healthy 16
Quiz 22
Key Words/Index 23
Log onto www.av2books.com 24

Chapter 1
What Are Muscles?

Think of the different ways you have moved today. Did you eat? Run down the stairs? Read the back of a cereal box? Use a pencil? Whisper to your friend? Frown over a hard math problem? If you did any of these things, then you used the muscles in your body.

Muscles are **tissues**. These tissues work to make your body move. They also help other organs in your body do their jobs. There are more than 600 muscles in your body. Some of these muscles move your bones. Others keep your heart beating or your lungs working. There are muscles in your eyes and in your stomach. Your tongue is also made of different muscles. These muscles help you talk and chew your food. Muscles in your face let you smile, frown, or look surprised.

The human arm has 23 muscle groups.

There are more than 50 muscles in your face. That is why you can make such funny faces.

Muscles 5

Muscles work by tightening and relaxing. You can try this activity right now. Place your right hand on the upper part of your left arm. Make a tight fist with your left hand. Can you feel how your muscles in the upper arm change? Now relax the left fist. Tighten and relax your fist a few more times. You can feel your muscles in your arm tightening and relaxing. This is how all muscles work.

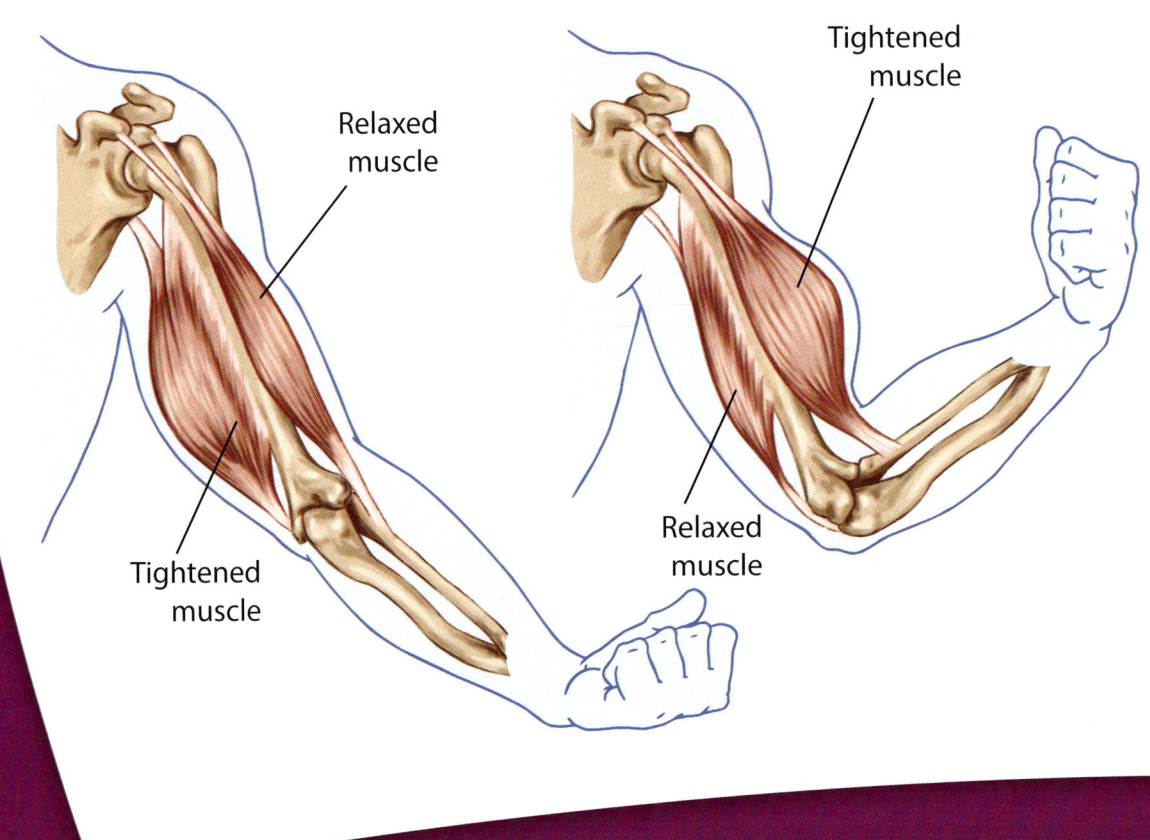

When the body moves or when heavy objects are lifted, you can feel the muscles working beneath the skin.

Chapter 2
Muscle Types

There are three types of muscles in your body. These types are **skeletal muscles, smooth muscles**, and the **cardiac muscle**. Skeletal muscles are **voluntary** muscles. This means you can control the muscles. You move your finger to hit a piano key. This uses a skeletal muscle attached to your finger. Skeletal muscles work with the bones to move the body. These muscles are attached to bones by a thin tissue called a tendon.

The muscle that controls your jaw is one of the strongest muscles. It is a skeletal muscle. Chewing food works the muscles in your jaw. The muscles in your jaw can close your teeth with more than 100 pounds (45 kilograms) of force.

Take a seat. You are now sitting on the biggest muscle in your body, the gluteus maximus.

Chewing uses a lot of muscles in the face.

Smooth muscles are **involuntary** muscles. These are muscles you have no control over. The pupil in your eye changes size when the light in a room changes. You cannot stop it because a smooth muscle controls the pupil. Smooth muscles are also found in organs that are hollow. This includes the stomach, small intestine, and bladder.

There are smooth muscles in your esophagus, too. The esophagus is the tube leading from your mouth into your stomach. There are many muscles at work whenever you swallow.

A cardiac muscle is also involuntary. This muscle is only found in the heart. The heart is one big muscle. When the heart muscle tightens, blood is sent out to the rest of the body. When the muscle relaxes, the heart fills with blood again. This muscle beats about 100,000 times each day and you never have to think about it.

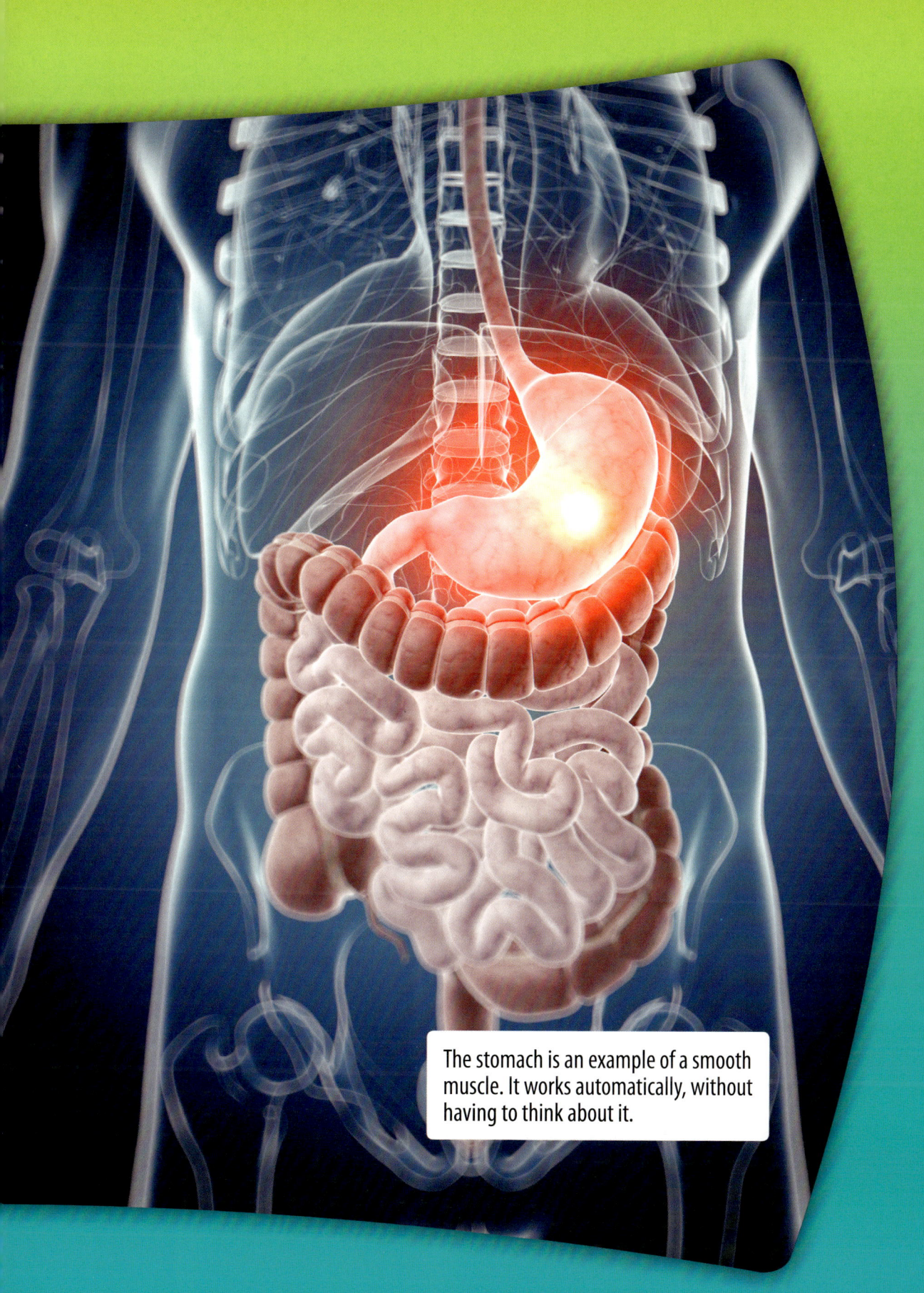

The stomach is an example of a smooth muscle. It works automatically, without having to think about it.

Chapter 3

Problems with Muscles

Chances are, your muscles feel sore from time to time. Your arm muscles may be sore after pitching several innings of a baseball game. You may feel soreness in your leg muscles after a long hike. Soreness in muscles is natural and usually does not mean something is wrong. Your muscles are simply getting stronger after being exercised.

Muscle **cramps** can hurt. A cramp is a sudden tightening of a muscle. Sometimes, the muscle feels hard when it is cramped. Cramps can happen with hard exercise or when a person does not drink enough water. Sometimes, cramps happen when there are vitamins missing from someone's diet. Stretching, using ice, and rubbing the muscle can usually help a cramp go away. One way to prevent cramps is to drink plenty of water.

When the body does new things, muscles can become sore.

Sometimes, a muscle becomes too stretched out. This is called a **strain**. A strain can happen suddenly. Lifting a heavy object may cause a strain to the back muscles. Strains can also happen slowly over time. Using the same muscles over and over to swing a tennis racket may lead to strain. The strained muscle may be too sore to use and may swell. Rest is the first step to healing the strained muscle. The muscle may need to be iced. Sometimes, wearing a bandage on the strained muscle can help, too.

Icing a strained muscle for 20 minutes each hour can help reduce the swelling.

It is important to stretch regularly. Warming up before working out and stretching afterwards can prevent strains.

A painful cramp in your calf is sometimes called a charley horse.

Muscles 15

Chapter 4
Keeping Your Muscles Healthy

You use your muscles every day, for almost everything you do. It is important to keep your muscles strong and healthy. One way to do that is by being active. Kids should try to exercise at least 60 minutes each day. Exercise makes muscles stronger. Running, jumping rope, or riding a bike are healthy things to do. Try out for a team sport. Being part of a team can be fun. It is a great way to make new friends, and keep your muscles healthy.

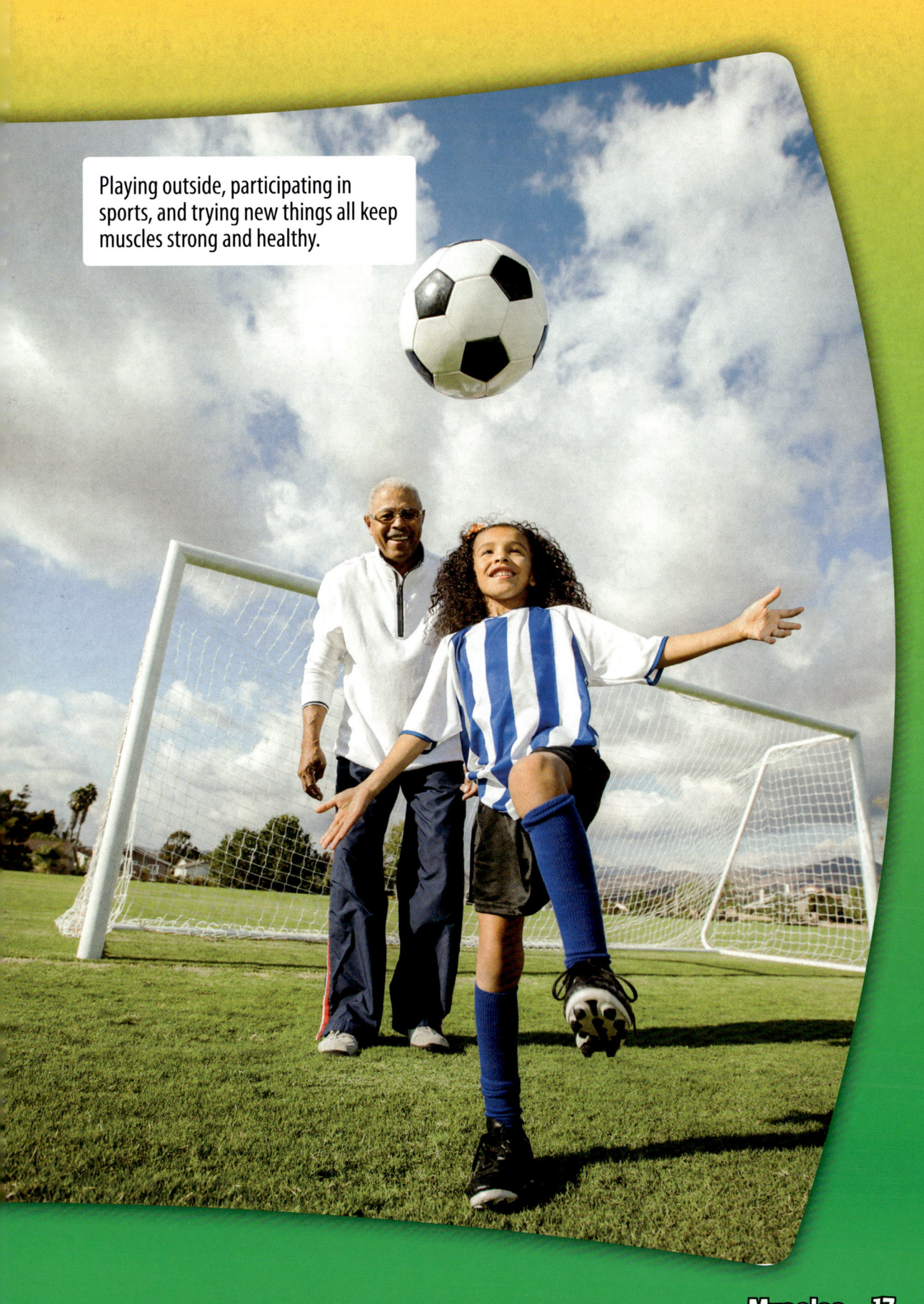

Playing outside, participating in sports, and trying new things all keep muscles strong and healthy.

Eating healthy foods can help your muscles. Eating fruits, vegetables, low-fat dairy, and lean meat help you stay at a healthy weight. Being at a healthy weight helps your muscles and bones work well. To help muscles grow, eat meats, beans, and eggs. Bananas and spinach have minerals that help muscles stay strong and healthy.

It is important to keep your muscles free from **injury**. There are things you can do before, during, and after exercise that will keep your muscles healthy. Always be sure to warm up before exercise and cool down afterward. Jog slowly before exercise to warm up your muscles. Cool down after exercise to keep your muscles from getting tight and sore. Cooling down means to slowly stop your exercise.

Protein helps build muscles. Eating a balanced diet that is high in protein can help keep the body strong.

Stretching helps strained muscles heal. It can also increase blood flow to the body.

You can break up your exercise into four 15-minute periods of time if you do not have an entire hour. Then you can try four different activities.

Be sure to use your muscles carefully. Practice good habits when lifting heavy objects to prevent strain. Lifting objects by bending your knees can help keep your back muscles healthy.

Always be sure to drink a lot of water before, during, and after exercise. Your muscles need water to stay strong. Drinking water, especially when the temperature is warm, will help avoid **dehydration**.

Pay attention to your body. Your muscles will tell you if there is a problem. Do not try to play through the pain during sports or exercise. You risk injury if you do not rest when your body is telling you to. Take good care of your muscles and they will keep you healthy and strong.

Muscles need a lot of water to work correctly. Experts say the body needs at least six glasses of water each day.

Quiz

1. How many muscles are in the human body?
2. What is the largest muscle in the body?
3. What are the three types of muscles in the body?
4. What is a cramp?
5. What is the only place in the body where the cardiac muscle is found?
6. What is a cramp in the calf sometimes called?
7. What can you do to keep your muscles free from injury during exercise?
8. How do muscles work?
9. How many muscles are in your face?
10. What type of muscles are in the esophagus?

Answers

1. More than 600
2. The gluteus maximus
3. Skeletal muscles, smooth muscles, and the cardiac muscle
4. A sudden tightening of a muscle
5. The heart
6. A charley horse
7. Warming up before exercise and cooling down afterward
8. By tightening and relaxing
9. More than 50
10. Smooth muscles

Key Words

cardiac muscle: a muscle found in the heart

cramps: a sudden tightening of a muscle

dehydration: occurs when more water is lost from the body than is taken in

injury: damage or harm to the body

involuntary: to have no control over something

skeletal muscles: muscles that are attached to bones and help move the body

smooth muscles: muscles found in the organs, such as the stomach

strain: stretching or tearing of a muscle or tendon

tissues: masses of cells with the same function

voluntary: to have control over something

Index

bones 4, 8, 18

cardiac muscle 8, 10
cramps 12, 15

dehydration 20

exercise 12, 16, 18, 19, 20

heart 4, 10

injury 18, 20
involuntary muscles 10

organs 4, 10

skeletal muscles 8
smooth muscles 8, 10, 11
soreness 12, 13, 14, 18
strain 14, 19, 20

tendons 8
tightened muscle 6, 10, 12, 18
tissues 4, 8

voluntary muscles 8

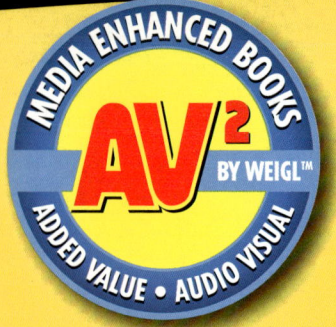

Log on to www.av2books.com

AV² by Weigl brings you media enhanced books that support active learning. Go to www.av2books.com, and enter the special code found on page 2 of this book. You will gain access to enriched and enhanced content that supplements and complements this book. Content includes video, audio, weblinks, quizzes, a slide show, and activities.

AV² Online Navigation

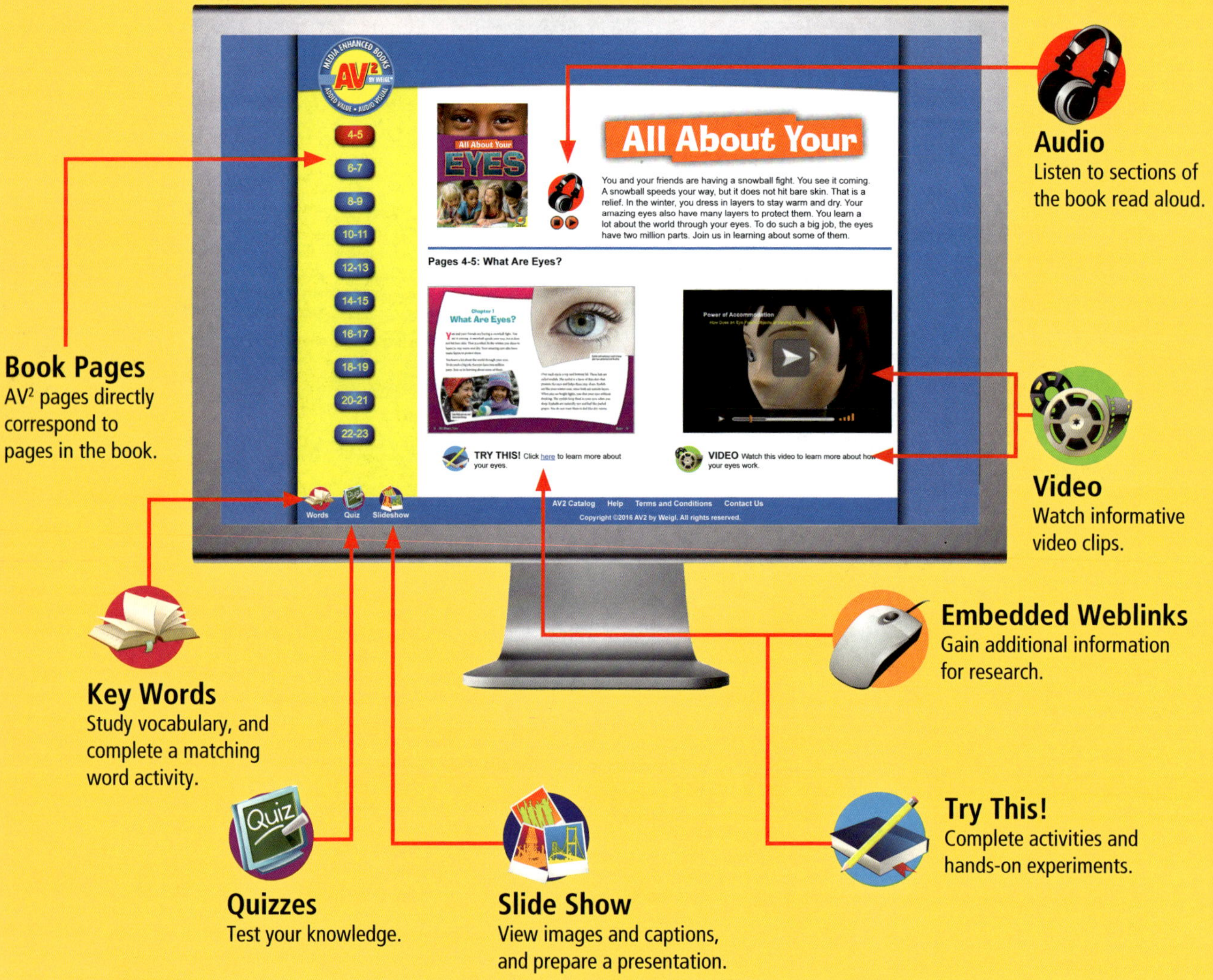

Audio
Listen to sections of the book read aloud.

Book Pages
AV² pages directly correspond to pages in the book.

Video
Watch informative video clips.

Embedded Weblinks
Gain additional information for research.

Key Words
Study vocabulary, and complete a matching word activity.

Try This!
Complete activities and hands-on experiments.

Quizzes
Test your knowledge.

Slide Show
View images and captions, and prepare a presentation.

AV² was built to bridge the gap between print and digital. We encourage you to tell us what you like and what you want to see in the future.

Sign up to be an AV² Ambassador at www.av2books.com/ambassador.

Due to the dynamic nature of the Internet, some of the URLs and activities provided as part of AV² by Weigl may have changed or ceased to exist. AV² by Weigl accepts no responsibility for any such changes. All media enhanced books are regularly monitored to update addresses and sites in a timely manner. Contact AV² by Weigl at 1-866-649-3445 or av2books@weigl.com with any questions, comments, or feedback.